THE PROTECTOR OF THE PAST

The Adventures of Daniel Thorne

Edimilson Franca

CONTENTS

Title Page

Introduction 2

Chapter 1: The Unveiling 6

Chapter 2: The Monastery's Secret 11

Chapter 3: The First Journey 17

Chapter 4: Echoes of Change 22

Chapter 5: Guardians and Betrayals 30

Chapter 6: Rebirth and Revolution 38

Chapter 7: Crossroads of Conflict 45

Chapter 8: Dawn of Innovation 51

Chapter 9: Echoes of Dissent 57

Chapter 10: The Cold War Conundrum 63

Chapter 11: The Digital Revolution 69

The Protector of the Past: The Adventures of Daniel Thorne

INTRODUCTION

In the heart of Europe, during the tumultuous year of 1347, the Black Death swept across the continent, leaving a trail of devastation in its wake. Entire villages were decimated, economies collapsed, and the social fabric of societies was torn apart. Amidst this chaos, a small monastery in the outskirts of what is now modern-day Germany, held a secret that could change the course of history. Hidden deep within its ancient walls, buried under centuries of dust and forgotten lore, was an artifact of unimaginable power: the Chrono Sphere.

The Chrono Sphere was no ordinary relic; it possessed the ability to manipulate the very fabric of time. Legends spoke of its creation by an enigmatic order of monks, who had sworn to protect it from falling into the wrong hands. This artifact, if wielded correctly, could alter the past, reshape the present, and even predict the future. Its immense power, however, came with a great responsibility, for it was said that those who dared to tamper with time would face dire consequences.

Centuries later, in the bustling city of London, a young historian named Daniel Thorne stumbled upon a cryptic manuscript in the dusty archives of the British Museum. Daniel, a brilliant but somewhat eccentric scholar, had always been fascinated by ancient mysteries and unsolved puzzles. His passion for history was rivaled only by his insatiable curiosity about time travel. The manuscript he discovered contained fragmented accounts of the Chrono Sphere and hinted at its last known location—the very monastery that had survived the ravages of the Black Death.

As Daniel delved deeper into the manuscript, he became increasingly convinced that the Chrono Sphere was real and that it held the key to unlocking the secrets of time. His mind raced with possibilities, envisioning a future where he could witness historical events firsthand, prevent catastrophic mistakes, and perhaps even change the course of his own troubled past. However, the more he learned about the artifact, the more he realized the dangers it posed. The manuscript warned of a shadowy organization known as the Temporal Order, a group of time-traveling zealots who sought to use the Chrono Sphere for their own nefarious purposes.

Driven by a sense of duty and an unyielding thirst for knowledge, Daniel embarked on a quest to uncover the truth about the Chrono Sphere. His journey took him from the hallowed halls of academia to the dark, winding streets of medieval Europe. Along the way, he encountered allies and adversaries, each with their own motivations and secrets. The stakes grew higher with every revelation, and Daniel soon found himself entangled in a web of intrigue, deception, and danger.

As Daniel navigated the treacherous waters of time travel, he grappled with ethical dilemmas and moral quandaries. Could he change the past without causing irreparable harm to the present? Would his actions have unforeseen consequences that could ripple through history? These questions weighed heavily on his mind, and he realized that the power to manipulate time came with an enormous responsibility.

In the monastery's shadowy corridors, Daniel uncovered hidden chambers and deciphered ancient codes, each step bringing him closer to the Chrono Sphere. His journey was fraught with peril, but he remained undeterred, driven by a sense of purpose and an unwavering belief in the importance of his mission. Along the way, he forged bonds with kindred spirits who shared his vision and supported his quest.

As the pieces of the puzzle began to fall into place, Daniel understood that his journey was about more than just discovering the Chrono Sphere. It was about protecting the fragile threads of history, ensuring that the lessons of the past were not forgotten, and safeguarding the future from those who sought to exploit time for their own gain. His adventure was a testament to the enduring power of knowledge, the resilience of the human spirit, and the timeless quest for truth and understanding.

The introduction of "The Protector of the Past: The Adventures of Daniel Thorne" sets the stage for an epic tale of mystery, adventure, and discovery. It immerses readers in a world where history and fantasy intertwine, creating an atmosphere of anticipation and excitement. As Daniel Thorne embarks on his quest, readers are invited to join him on a journey through time, where every chapter promises new revelations, challenges, and triumphs.

CHAPTER 1: THE UNVEILING

The British Museum, with its grandiose halls and countless artifacts, had always been a second home to Daniel Thorne. On a particularly rainy afternoon, Daniel found himself tucked away in a forgotten corner of the museum's vast archives. The dimly lit room, filled with the scent of old parchment and leather, was his sanctuary—a place where he could lose himself in the pages of history.

It was here, amidst stacks of dusty tomes, that Daniel discovered the manuscript that would change his life forever. Bound in cracked leather and written in an archaic script, the manuscript exuded an aura of mystery and significance. His fingers trembled as he carefully opened it, revealing pages filled with cryptic symbols, drawings of intricate machinery, and fragmented accounts of an object called the Chrono Sphere.

Intrigued, Daniel spent hours deciphering the manuscript, his eyes widening with each revelation. The Chrono Sphere, according to the text, was an artifact of immense power capable of manipulating time itself. The monks who created it had done so to safeguard history from those who would seek to alter its course. But the manuscript also warned of a dark force—the Temporal Order—intent on harnessing the Chrono Sphere for their own sinister purposes.

Daniel's heart raced as he read about the Temporal Order, a secretive organization that had manipulated events throughout history to further their own agenda. The manuscript recounted tales of assassinations, wars, and other catastrophic events orchestrated by the Order. Their influence spanned centuries, and their reach was global. The Chrono Sphere, it seemed, was the key to their power, and they would stop at nothing to reclaim it.

The weight of his discovery settled heavily on Daniel's shoulders. He knew that he couldn't keep this knowledge to himself. The potential for misuse was too great, and the consequences too dire. He needed to find the Chrono Sphere before the Temporal Order did. But where to start? The manuscript hinted at the artifact's last known location: a monastery on the outskirts of Germany, untouched by time.

Determined, Daniel packed his belongings and booked the earliest flight to Germany. His journey was shrouded in secrecy; he told no one of his plans, fearing that the Temporal Order might already be aware of his discovery. The flight was long and uneventful, giving him ample time to pore over the manuscript again and again, memorizing every detail.

Upon arriving in Germany, Daniel rented a car and drove through the picturesque countryside, his eyes scanning the horizon for any sign of the monastery. The manuscript described it as a place hidden from the world, its location known only to a select few. As he navigated narrow, winding roads and dense forests, a sense of unease settled over him. He was venturing into the unknown, armed only with his wits and the cryptic clues from an ancient text.

After hours of searching, Daniel finally glimpsed the monastery. Nestled atop a hill and surrounded by a thick grove of trees, it stood as a testament to time's passage. The building was imposing, with tall, weathered walls and narrow windows that seemed to gaze out like the eyes of a guardian. Daniel approached cautiously, his steps echoing on the cobblestone path leading to the entrance.

The monastery's interior was as austere as its exterior. Cold stone floors and bare walls gave way to long corridors lined with wooden doors. The air was thick with silence, broken only by the distant sound of chanting monks. Daniel moved with purpose, guided by the manuscript's descriptions. He knew he had to find the hidden chamber mentioned in the text—the chamber where the Chrono Sphere was said to be kept.

Navigating the labyrinthine passages, Daniel felt a growing sense of urgency. Each step brought him closer to the heart of the mystery, but also closer to danger. The Temporal Order could be anywhere, watching, waiting. He couldn't afford to make a mistake. Finally, he reached a door adorned with intricate carvings, the same symbols he'd seen in the manuscript. His breath caught in his throat as he pushed it open.

Inside, the room was bathed in a soft, ethereal light. Ancient manuscripts and relics filled the shelves, but at the center stood a pedestal, upon which rested the Chrono Sphere. It was smaller than he had imagined, fitting easily into the palm of his hand, but its surface shimmered with a mesmerizing glow. As Daniel reached out to touch it, he felt a surge of energy course through him, a connection to the very fabric of time.

In that moment, he understood the true power of the Chrono Sphere. It was more than just a tool; it was a guardian of history, a beacon of knowledge, and a weapon against those who sought to corrupt time. Holding it in his hands, Daniel felt the weight of his responsibility. He had to protect the Chrono Sphere from the Temporal Order and use it to safeguard the past, present, and future.

But as he turned to leave, a shadowy figure emerged from the darkness, blocking his path. The man's eyes gleamed with malice, and a cruel smile played on his lips. "I've been waiting for you, Mr. Thorne," he said, his voice dripping with menace. "The Temporal Order sends its regards."

Daniel's heart pounded in his chest as he realized the danger he was in. The quest for the Chrono Sphere had only just begun, and already, he was facing his first real test. With the artifact clutched tightly in his hand, he prepared to confront his adversary, knowing that the fate of history itself hung in the balance.

CHAPTER 2: THE MONASTERY'S SECRET

The shadowy figure stepped closer, his presence filling the room with an oppressive weight. Daniel's mind raced, trying to recall every detail from the manuscript that might help him in this confrontation. The Temporal Order was relentless, and this man was likely just the first of many obstacles he would face.

"Who are you?" Daniel demanded, his voice steady despite the fear that churned within him.

The man smirked. "My name is Lucius, an agent of the Temporal Order. And you, Mr. Thorne, are meddling in affairs far beyond your understanding."

Daniel tightened his grip on the Chrono Sphere. "I'm

not here to cause harm. I want to protect history, not alter it."

Lucius's eyes narrowed. "You naive fool. History is meant to be controlled, shaped by those with the wisdom to wield such power. Hand over the Chrono Sphere, and perhaps I'll let you leave this place unharmed."

Daniel knew he couldn't trust Lucius. He had to think quickly. "Why does the Temporal Order want the Chrono Sphere? What are you planning to do with it?"

Lucius laughed, a cold, mirthless sound. "You think you can stall me with questions? Our plans are none of your concern. Now, give me the Sphere."

With a sudden burst of resolve, Daniel made his move. He lunged forward, using the element of surprise to his advantage. Lucius was quick, but Daniel's desperation fueled his speed. He knocked Lucius off balance and dashed towards the door, the Chrono Sphere clutched tightly in his hand.

The corridors of the monastery blurred past as Daniel ran, his footsteps echoing off the stone walls. He could hear Lucius's pursuit behind him, growing louder with each passing second. Daniel's mind raced, searching for a way out. The manuscript had mentioned a hidden exit, a passage used by the monks in times of danger. If he could find it, he might have a chance to escape.

Turning a corner, Daniel spotted a small alcove with a carved symbol matching one from the manuscript. He pressed his hand against it, and to his relief, the wall slid open, revealing a narrow, dark passage. He slipped inside just as Lucius rounded the corner, missing him by mere seconds.

The passage was cramped and filled with cobwebs, but Daniel pressed on, the Chrono Sphere illuminating the way. His breaths came in short gasps, but he forced himself to keep moving. The manuscript had said the passage would lead to a hidden chapel, a sanctuary where the monks had once sought refuge.

After what felt like an eternity, Daniel emerged into the chapel. It was a small, serene space, with stained glass windows casting colorful patterns on the floor. He paused to catch his breath, his eyes scanning the room for any sign of danger. For the moment, it seemed he was safe.

But he couldn't stay here. Lucius and the Temporal Order would stop at nothing to retrieve the Chrono Sphere. He needed to find allies, people who understood the gravity of the situation and could help him protect the artifact.

As he contemplated his next move, Daniel heard a soft rustling sound. He turned to see an elderly monk standing in the shadows, his eyes filled with a mix of curiosity and concern.

"Who are you?" the monk asked, his voice gentle but firm.

"My name is Daniel Thorne," Daniel replied, still catching his breath. "I found the Chrono Sphere, and now the Temporal Order is after me. I need your help."

The monk stepped forward, his gaze fixed on the glowing artifact in Daniel's hand. "The Chrono Sphere," he murmured. "It has been centuries since anyone has laid eyes on it. You are in grave danger, my son. The Temporal Order will stop at nothing to obtain it."

"I know," Daniel said, desperation creeping into his voice. "But I can't do this alone. I need to understand more about the Sphere and how to protect it."

The monk nodded solemnly. "Follow me, then. There is much you need to learn, and time is of the essence."

He led Daniel through a hidden door at the back of the chapel, down a spiraling staircase that seemed to descend into the very heart of the earth. The air grew cooler and more oppressive with each step, but Daniel pressed on, driven by the urgency of his mission.

At the bottom of the staircase, they entered a vast underground chamber. Ancient tomes and scrolls lined the walls, and the air was thick with the scent of aged parchment. In the center of the room stood an ornate pedestal, upon which rested a large, ancient book.

The monk gestured to the book. "This is the Codex Temporis, the Book of Time. It contains all the knowledge and wisdom of those who have guarded the Chrono Sphere throughout the ages. You must study it, understand its teachings, and prepare yourself for the trials ahead."

Daniel approached the pedestal, his hands trembling as he opened the book. The pages were filled with intricate illustrations, complex diagrams, and passages written in a language he barely understood. But as he began to read, he felt a sense of clarity and purpose. This was the key to unlocking the true power of the Chrono Sphere and protecting it from those who sought to abuse it.

The monk placed a reassuring hand on Daniel's shoulder. "You are now the protector of the Chrono Sphere, Daniel Thorne. Your journey will be fraught with danger, but you are not alone. We, the Guardians of Time, will aid you in your quest. Together, we will ensure that history remains untainted and that the future is preserved for all mankind."

As Daniel immersed himself in the Codex Temporis, he felt a renewed sense of determination. He was no longer just a historian or a curious scholar; he was a guardian of time, entrusted with the most powerful artifact in history. The path ahead was uncertain, but he knew that he had the strength, the knowledge, and the allies he needed to face whatever challenges lay in store.

And so, with the Chrono Sphere in one hand and the wisdom of the Codex Temporis in the other, Daniel Thorne prepared to embark on the greatest adventure of his life—a journey through time itself, where every decision could change the course of history and shape the destiny of humanity.

CHAPTER 3: THE FIRST JOURNEY

The underground chamber buzzed with an air of ancient power and unspoken secrets. As Daniel absorbed the wisdom contained within the Codex Temporis, the reality of his mission settled in. The room's flickering torchlight cast shadows that danced on the stone walls, creating an almost ethereal ambiance.

Brother Mathias, the elderly monk who had first greeted Daniel, stood by his side, his presence a comforting reminder that Daniel was not alone in this endeavor. "The Codex Temporis will guide you, Daniel. But it's crucial that you practice caution. The Chrono Sphere's power is immense, and its use must be judicious."

Daniel nodded, feeling the weight of responsibility more than ever. "Where do I begin? The manuscript mentioned key historical events influenced by the Temporal Order. How do I know where to go first?"

Brother Mathias stroked his beard thoughtfully. "There is one event that stands out, a moment in history that the Temporal Order has been known to covet—the assassination of Archduke Franz Ferdinand in 1914. His death ignited the spark that led to World War I, a war that reshaped the world."

Daniel felt a chill run down his spine. Preventing such an assassination could change the course of history in profound ways. But could he alter such a pivotal event without catastrophic consequences? "If I'm to intervene, how do I ensure I'm doing the right thing? What if my actions cause more harm than good?"

Brother Mathias's eyes bore into Daniel's, filled with the gravity of centuries-old wisdom. "That is the burden of your role, Daniel. You must act not out of personal desire, but with the greater good in mind. The Codex will help you understand the flow of time and the consequences of your actions. Trust in it, and in yourself."

With a deep breath, Daniel placed the Chrono Sphere on the pedestal next to the Codex. As he concentrated, the Sphere began to glow brighter, its energy pulsating in harmony with the ancient book. The room around him seemed to blur and shift, the boundaries of time dissolving as the Chrono Sphere transported him to a different era.

Daniel found himself in Sarajevo, the air heavy with anticipation and unease. The year was 1914, and the city was a boiling pot of political tension. The streets were bustling, filled with the sights and sounds of a world on the brink of monumental change. He adjusted his clothing to blend in—a simple suit and hat that would allow him to move through the crowd unnoticed.

He had studied this moment extensively: June 28, 1914, the day Archduke Franz Ferdinand and his wife, Sophie, were to be assassinated. The details were etched in his mind, but seeing it unfold in real time was a different experience altogether. He had one goal: to prevent the assassination without causing a ripple effect that could destabilize the future.

As he navigated through the throngs of people, Daniel's mind raced. He needed to identify the key players—the Black Hand assassins led by Gavrilo Princip. He had learned their movements, their plans, and their positions from historical records. Now, he had to put that knowledge to use.

Near the Latin Bridge, Daniel spotted Princip lurking in the shadows, waiting for the Archduke's motorcade. The tension was palpable, and every second counted. Daniel edged closer, keeping a careful eye on the young assassin. He knew that one misstep could alert Princip and ruin his chance to intervene.

Suddenly, the sound of engines grew louder as the Archduke's car approached. Daniel's heart pounded. He had to act now. With swift, calculated movements, he positioned himself between Princip and the car, ensuring that any attempt at the assassination would be thwarted.

The car slowed as it approached the corner, and in that instant, Daniel made his move. He lunged towards Princip, knocking the gun from his hand just as he aimed at the Archduke. Chaos erupted as the crowd realized what was happening. Shouts and screams filled the air, but Daniel remained focused, ensuring Princip was subdued.

The Archduke's car sped away, its passengers shaken but unharmed. Daniel quickly slipped into the crowd, knowing he had altered the course of history. The questions of what consequences his actions would bring weighed heavily on his mind, but he pushed them aside for now. He had done what he believed was right.

Returning to the present was a disorienting experience. The monastery's chamber came back into focus, the Codex Temporis and the Chrono Sphere pulsing gently as if acknowledging his success. Brother Mathias awaited him, eyes filled with a mix of concern and curiosity.

"Did you succeed?" Mathias asked.

Daniel nodded, though uncertainty still lingered. "I stopped the assassination. But I don't know what the repercussions will be."

Brother Mathias placed a reassuring hand on his shoulder. "You've taken the first step, Daniel. The future is always in flux, shaped by our actions and decisions. Trust in your judgment, and remember that you are not alone. We are here to guide you."

Daniel took a deep breath, feeling a sense of accomplishment mingled with apprehension. His journey was only beginning, and the path ahead was fraught with challenges and unknowns. But he was determined to protect history, to ensure that the past remained untainted and that the future was safeguarded for generations to come.

As he stood in the ancient chamber, surrounded by the wisdom of the ages, Daniel Thorne knew that he was ready to face whatever trials lay ahead. The Chrono Sphere's power was both a gift and a burden, but with it, he had the means to make a difference—a protector of the past, and a guardian of the future.

CHAPTER 4: ECHOES OF CHANGE

The echoes of Daniel's first mission reverberated through the monastery's ancient halls. While he had successfully prevented the assassination of Archduke Franz Ferdinand, the implications of his actions remained uncertain. The Codex Temporis offered no guarantees, only guidance, and it was up to Daniel to navigate the complexities of time.

Brother Mathias observed Daniel as he studied the Codex, a mixture of pride and concern in his eyes. "Every action in the past has consequences, Daniel. Some we can foresee, others we cannot. But remember, your intentions were noble. You acted to preserve life and prevent chaos."

Daniel nodded, though the weight of responsibility

still pressed heavily on him. "I just hope I haven't made things worse. The Temporal Order won't stop, and neither can I."

Mathias smiled gently. "You've taken your first step into a much larger world. The Codex will help you understand the flow of time and its many branches. For now, rest and gather your strength. There are more challenges ahead."

Days turned into weeks as Daniel immersed himself in the Codex, its pages revealing secrets of time manipulation, historical events, and the philosophies of the ancient monks who had protected the Chrono Sphere for centuries. The more he learned, the more he realized how delicate the balance of history truly was.

One evening, as Daniel pored over a particularly complex passage, Brother Mathias approached him with a look of urgency. "Daniel, there is something you must see."

They made their way to a secluded chamber deep within the monastery. Inside, an array of maps and documents were spread across a large table. Mathias pointed to a specific map, its edges frayed and worn. "This is a map of Europe during the 18th century. There have been reports of anomalies in this era, specifically around the time of the American Revolution."

Daniel's eyes widened. "The American Revolution? But that was a pivotal moment in history. If the Temporal Order is meddling with it—"

"Exactly," Mathias interrupted. "If they alter the outcome, the entire course of modern history could be changed. We must act swiftly."

Daniel felt a surge of determination. "I'll go. But I need to know more about what I'm facing. The Revolution was a complex event with many key figures and battles."

Mathias handed Daniel a stack of documents. "These are reports we've gathered from various sources. Study them carefully. You must be prepared for anything."

As Daniel delved into the documents, he felt a familiar blend of excitement and apprehension. The American Revolution was a time of great upheaval and change. The stakes were high, and the potential for disaster immense. But he was ready to face the challenge.

The journey to 1776 was smoother this time. Daniel felt a growing sense of confidence in his abilities, bolstered by his studies and the support of the Guardians of Time. When he emerged from the temporal shift, he found himself in a bustling colonial town. The air was thick with anticipation and the spirit of rebellion.

He had arrived in Boston, a city at the heart of the revolutionary fervor. The streets were alive with activity, merchants peddling their goods, soldiers marching, and citizens whispering about the latest actions of the British and the Patriots. Daniel knew he needed to find key figures in the Revolution—individuals whose actions would shape the future.

His first destination was a tavern known to be a gathering place for revolutionary leaders. As he entered, the warm glow of lanterns and the hum of conversation enveloped him. He spotted a group of men in the corner, deep in discussion. Among them were John Adams, Samuel Adams, and Paul Revere—icons of the American Revolution.

Daniel approached cautiously, knowing he needed to earn their trust without revealing too much. "Excuse me, gentlemen. My name is Daniel Thorne. I'm a historian from... abroad. I've come to offer my assistance in your cause."

The men exchanged wary glances, but John Adams spoke up. "We welcome all who are dedicated to the cause of liberty. What brings you to Boston, Mr. Thorne?"

Daniel took a deep breath, choosing his words carefully. "I've studied your struggle extensively. I believe I can offer insights and support that may prove valuable in the days to come."

Samuel Adams narrowed his eyes. "And what kind of support might that be?"

Daniel leaned in, lowering his voice. "Information. I have knowledge of the British plans, their movements, and strategies. I can help you stay one step ahead."

The men looked skeptical, but Paul Revere's interest was piqued. "If what you say is true, Mr. Thorne, then you may indeed be a valuable ally. But understand this—we are fighting for our lives, our freedom. Any false move could cost us dearly."

Daniel nodded solemnly. "I understand. I only ask for a chance to prove myself."

The next few days were a whirlwind of activity. Daniel integrated himself into the revolutionary efforts, providing crucial intelligence that helped the Patriots anticipate British maneuvers. His knowledge of historical events proved invaluable, allowing the revolutionaries to make strategic decisions that bolstered their position.

However, as the days passed, Daniel couldn't shake the feeling that the Temporal Order was watching. He knew they wouldn't simply abandon their plans. They would adapt, and they would strike when least expected.

One evening, as Daniel walked through the dimly lit streets of Boston, he sensed he was being followed. He quickened his pace, turning down an alley in an attempt to lose his pursuer. But when he reached the end, a figure stepped out of the shadows, blocking his path.

"Daniel Thorne," the man said, his voice dripping with malice. "Did you really think you could outsmart the Temporal Order?"

Daniel's heart raced as he recognized Lucius, the same agent he had encountered in the monastery. "What do you want, Lucius?"

Lucius smirked. "You may have delayed us, but you can't stop us. The Chrono Sphere belongs to us, and we will reclaim it. You have no idea the forces you're dealing with."

Before Daniel could react, Lucius lunged at him, a dagger glinting in his hand. The two men grappled in the narrow alley, their struggle fierce and desperate. Daniel fought with every ounce of strength he had, determined to protect the Chrono Sphere and the future it safeguarded.

In a final, desperate move, Daniel managed to disarm Lucius, sending the dagger clattering to the ground. Lucius snarled in frustration, but Daniel held his ground. "This isn't over, Thorne. The

Temporal Order will find you, and when we do, you'll wish you had never meddled in our affairs."

With that, Lucius disappeared into the shadows, leaving Daniel to catch his breath and gather his thoughts. The encounter had shaken him, but it had also steeled his resolve. The Temporal Order was relentless, but so was he.

Back in the sanctuary of the monastery, Daniel recounted his experience to Brother Mathias. The elder monk listened intently, his expression grave. "The Temporal Order's influence is stronger than we anticipated. You did well, Daniel, but we must remain vigilant."

Daniel nodded. "I know. They won't stop until they have the Chrono Sphere. But I won't let them succeed. We have to keep fighting, protecting history from their grasp."

Brother Mathias placed a hand on Daniel's shoulder. "You are not alone in this fight. The Guardians of Time will support you, and together, we will preserve the integrity of history. Remember, Daniel, the path you walk is fraught with danger, but it is also one of great honor and purpose."

As Daniel prepared for his next journey, he felt a renewed sense of determination. The challenges were immense, and the stakes higher than ever. But with the Chrono Sphere and the wisdom of the

Codex Temporis at his side, he was ready to face whatever the future—and the past—had in store.

The adventure continued, with Daniel Thorne as its steadfast protector, navigating the intricate tapestry of time and ensuring that history remained untainted by those who sought to control it.

CHAPTER 5: GUARDIANS AND BETRAYALS

Days turned into nights as Daniel delved deeper into the mysteries of the Codex Temporis. Each passage revealed new layers of knowledge, guiding him through the labyrinth of history. The monastery, once a place of solace, now felt like a strategic headquarters, buzzing with activity and purpose.

Brother Mathias remained a steadfast mentor, but Daniel couldn't ignore the growing tension among the Guardians. Whispers of betrayal and distrust echoed through the ancient halls, hinting at cracks within their ranks. Daniel knew that unity was crucial, but the weight of his recent encounters with the Temporal Order hung heavily over him.

One evening, as Daniel studied the Codex, Brother

Mathias entered the chamber, his expression grim. "Daniel, there's something you need to know. We've received intelligence that the Temporal Order has infiltrated our ranks. We have a traitor among us."

Daniel's heart sank. "Who could it be? We've all sworn to protect the Chrono Sphere."

Mathias shook his head. "We don't know yet, but we must be vigilant. Trust is a fragile thing, and the Temporal Order will exploit any weakness they find."

Determined to uncover the traitor, Daniel began observing his fellow Guardians more closely. Each interaction, every subtle gesture, became a potential clue. It was a delicate balance—seeking the truth without sowing further discord.

Weeks passed, and tensions within the monastery reached a boiling point. Daniel's investigations had yielded little concrete evidence, but he remained vigilant. One night, as he wandered the silent corridors, he overheard hushed voices coming from a hidden alcove.

He approached cautiously, straining to hear the conversation. "We can't keep this up," one voice said, tinged with desperation. "The Temporal Order's promises are tempting, but betraying the Guardians? It's too risky."

Another voice responded, calmer and more resolute. "We have no choice. The Temporal Order will win, and we must be on the right side of history. Besides, the power they offer is beyond anything we've dreamed of."

Daniel's blood ran cold. He recognized the voices —two of his fellow Guardians, Elias and Marcellus. The betrayal was real, and it was closer than he had imagined. Taking a deep breath, Daniel stepped into the alcove, his presence startling the conspirators.

"Elias, Marcellus," Daniel said, his voice steady despite the turmoil within him. "I trusted you. We all did."

Elias's eyes widened with fear, but Marcellus remained defiant. "You're a fool, Daniel. The Temporal Order will reshape history, and we'll be part of that new world. Join us, or be swept aside."

Daniel shook his head. "I can't betray everything we stand for. The Chrono Sphere is meant to protect history, not control it. Don't you see the danger in what you're doing?"

Marcellus sneered. "You're naive. History is written by the victors. The Temporal Order understands that, and soon, so will you."

Before Daniel could react, Marcellus lunged at him. The two men grappled, their struggle intense and desperate. Elias hesitated, torn between loyalty and fear, but ultimately chose to flee, disappearing into the shadows.

With a final, decisive move, Daniel overpowered Marcellus, pinning him to the ground. "It's over, Marcellus. The Guardians will not fall to the Temporal Order."

Marcellus glared up at him, his eyes filled with a mix of rage and resignation. "You may have won this battle, Thorne, but the war is far from over. The Temporal Order is everywhere, and they will find you."

The following day, Daniel and Brother Mathias confronted the remaining Guardians, revealing the betrayal and the confrontation. The news shook the group, but it also solidified their resolve. They had faced betrayal from within, but they were united in their mission.

"Trust must be rebuilt," Mathias said, addressing the gathered Guardians. "We have faced a grave threat, but we must remain strong. Our duty to protect the Chrono Sphere and the integrity of history is paramount."

Daniel nodded in agreement. "We must be vigilant, but we cannot let fear divide us. The Temporal Order is relentless, but so are we. Together, we will ensure that history remains untainted."

The Guardians reaffirmed their commitment, their unity stronger than before. But Daniel knew that the battle against the Temporal Order was far from over. The stakes were higher than ever, and the enemy more cunning and ruthless.

As Daniel prepared for his next journey, the Codex Temporis revealed a new chapter—a series of events surrounding the fall of the Roman Empire. The Temporal Order's influence had been detected in this era, and Daniel's mission was clear: to safeguard one of the most pivotal moments in history.

The journey through time was becoming second nature to him. The Chrono Sphere's power felt like an extension of himself, guiding him through the intricate web of past events. When he arrived in ancient Rome, the city was a blend of grandeur and decay, its glory days slipping away as internal strife and external threats mounted.

Daniel's target was a senator named Quintus, a key figure whose decisions would shape the fate of the empire. The Temporal Order sought to manipulate him, ensuring the empire's fall would be expedited and chaotic, creating a power vacuum they could exploit.

Navigating the political landscape of ancient Rome was no easy task. Daniel had to be cautious, using his knowledge of history and the insights from the

Codex to influence events subtly. He posed as a scholar from a distant land, gaining access to the Senate and earning Quintus's trust.

In his interactions with Quintus, Daniel emphasized the importance of unity and strategic alliances, hoping to sway the senator's decisions towards stability rather than conflict. It was a delicate dance, balancing his intervention with the need to preserve the natural flow of history.

One evening, as Daniel discussed the empire's future with Quintus, he sensed a familiar presence. Lucius, ever the shadowy adversary, had followed him to Rome. The Temporal Order's reach was vast, and their determination unyielding.

Lucius approached, his smile a sinister mask. "You never learn, do you, Thorne? Always meddling where you don't belong."

Daniel stood his ground. "I'm here to protect history, Lucius. The Temporal Order's ambitions will lead to chaos and ruin."

Lucius laughed. "History is already chaotic. We're just guiding it towards a future where we hold the reins."

Their confrontation drew the attention of the Senate, and Daniel knew he had to act quickly. With Quintus watching, he needed to expose Lucius's true intentions without revealing the existence of the Chrono Sphere.

"Quintus," Daniel said, turning to the senator. "This man seeks to manipulate you for his own gain. He represents a faction that thrives on chaos and destruction."

Lucius's smile faltered. "Don't listen to him, Quintus. He's an outsider with no understanding of our struggles."

Quintus frowned, his gaze shifting between the two men. "What proof do you have, Daniel?"

Daniel took a deep breath, choosing his words carefully. "I have seen the consequences of his actions in other lands. Wherever he goes, instability follows. His promises are empty, and his allegiance is to power, not to Rome."

The Senate murmured, tension thick in the air. Quintus studied Lucius, doubt flickering in his eyes. "Is this true? Are you here to sow discord?"

Lucius's facade cracked, his anger simmering beneath the surface. "I am here to ensure Rome's future. A future where we are strong and unchallenged."

Daniel seized the moment. "A future built on deceit and manipulation is no future at all. Rome's strength lies in its people, in unity and honor."

Quintus nodded slowly, his decision made. "Guards, remove this man. He has no place in our Senate."

As Lucius was escorted away, his eyes locked onto Daniel's, a promise of retribution burning in their depths. The victory was a small one, but it reinforced Daniel's resolve.

Back at the monastery, Daniel shared his success with Brother Mathias and the Guardians. They had won another battle, but the war against the Temporal Order raged on. Each mission brought new challenges and dangers, but it also strengthened their bond and their commitment to protecting history.

"Your journey is far from over, Daniel," Mathias said, his voice a mix of pride and caution. "The Temporal Order will not relent, and neither can we. But remember, you are not alone. We stand with you, as Guardians of Time."

Daniel nodded, the weight of his mission ever-present but his determination unwavering. He was ready to face whatever the past—and the future—had in store, guided by the Codex Temporis and the strength of his allies. The adventures of Daniel Thorne continued, a protector of the past, and a guardian of the future.

CHAPTER 6: REBIRTH AND REVOLUTION

The monastery's halls, now echoing with newfound resolve, provided Daniel a brief respite from the ceaseless challenges of time travel. Each success and setback sharpened his focus, as the Temporal Order's schemes grew more audacious. Daniel knew that the next mission would test him in ways he had yet to experience.

The Codex Temporis guided him to a tumultuous period: the French Revolution. This era, rife with conflict and transformation, was a crucial battleground for the Temporal Order. Their aim was clear—manipulate the revolution to ensure that chaos and instability would weaken the forces of progress and potentially reshape the modern world to their advantage.

As Daniel stepped into the heart of revolutionary France, he was struck by the stark contrast between the grandeur of the past and the reality of the present. The streets of Paris were a chaotic mix of fervent revolutionaries and wary citizens. The air was thick with the promise of change and the threat of violence.

His mission was twofold: to protect key figures in the revolution who were crucial to maintaining the course of history and to prevent the Temporal Order from exploiting the revolution's chaos.

In the crowded marketplace, Daniel blended in as a trader from a neighboring country. His knowledge of French history and culture allowed him to move among the people, gathering information and assessing the situation. His primary target was Maximilien Robespierre, a leading figure in the revolutionary government whose decisions would significantly influence the revolution's outcome.

The Codex Temporis provided insights into Robespierre's critical moments, highlighting decisions that would shape France's future. Daniel had to ensure Robespierre stayed true to his vision of a republic based on principles of liberty and equality, rather than succumbing to the extreme measures that could be manipulated by the Temporal Order.

One evening, Daniel managed to secure a meeting with Robespierre under the guise of offering support to the revolutionary cause. The setting was a modest but well-furnished room, filled with revolutionary documents and maps. Robespierre, a man of sharp intellect and steely resolve, scrutinized Daniel with a mixture of suspicion and curiosity.

"Who are you, and what brings you to my doorstep at such a critical time?" Robespierre demanded, his voice laced with urgency.

Daniel remained composed. "I am Daniel Thorne, a supporter of the revolutionary ideals. I come with information and resources that may aid in securing the revolution's goals."

Robespierre's gaze remained piercing. "Information? And what exactly can you provide that we do not already know?"

Daniel took a deep breath. "I have knowledge of potential threats—both internal and external. There are those who seek to exploit the revolution's turmoil for their own gain, including factions that wish to control the outcome of our struggle."

Robespierre's expression shifted from skepticism to interest. "You speak of manipulation. What evidence do you have of this?"

Daniel reached into his bag and retrieved documents he had acquired through careful observation and discreet sources. "These documents detail covert operations and communications from groups that wish to undermine our efforts. They aim to destabilize the revolution from within and create a power vacuum that benefits them."

Robespierre reviewed the documents, his eyes narrowing as he absorbed the information. "If what you say is true, then our struggle is at risk from within as well as from outside forces. We cannot afford to be complacent."

With Robespierre's attention focused, Daniel used the opportunity to emphasize the importance of unity and vigilance. "Your leadership is crucial, Maximilien. The revolution's success depends on a balanced approach—one that upholds its core principles while effectively countering threats."

As the conversation continued, Daniel felt the weight of responsibility. His role was not to lead or make decisions, but to provide support and ensure the integrity of the revolution's trajectory. The revolution was a fragile entity, its future contingent on the decisions made by its leaders.

The Temporal Order, however, was relentless. Daniel's presence did not go unnoticed. One night, while walking through the narrow, dimly lit streets of Paris, he sensed the familiar presence of Lucius and other agents of the Temporal Order. The confrontation was inevitable.

Daniel ducked into a hidden alley, hoping to lose his pursuers. But Lucius was relentless, emerging from the shadows with an air of confidence. "You're becoming quite the thorn in our side, Thorne. Do you really believe you can alter the course of history with your meddling?"

Daniel stood his ground, drawing upon his resolve. "I'm here to protect the revolution and ensure that it remains true to its ideals. You and your Order will not undermine it."

Lucius smirked. "The revolution is already a breeding ground for chaos. Our influence only accelerates what is inevitable. The question is not whether we will succeed, but how much you can delay it."

A fierce battle ensued in the shadows, the clash of ideals and physical combat intertwining. Daniel fought with determination, driven by his commitment to safeguarding history. Despite his efforts, Lucius and his agents managed to escape, leaving behind a sense of urgency and renewed determination in Daniel.

Back at the monastery, Daniel reported on his experiences, sharing his insights and the continued threat posed by the Temporal Order. The Guardians listened intently, their resolve hardened by the knowledge of the Order's persistent interference.

"The revolution is a turning point," Brother Mathias said, his tone grave. "We must remain vigilant. The Order's tactics will only grow more sophisticated, and our responses must be equally adept."

Daniel nodded. "We have faced betrayal and conflict, but our mission remains clear. We must protect history from those who seek to control it for their own ends."

The Codex Temporis revealed the next chapter of Daniel's journey: a critical moment in the American Civil War. The Temporal Order sought to exploit this era's divisions, aiming to alter the outcome of the war and manipulate its consequences.

As Daniel prepared for his next mission, he reflected on the challenges he had faced and the battles yet to come. The struggle against the Temporal Order was far from over, but with the Codex Temporis and the support of the Guardians, he was ready to confront whatever trials awaited him.

The adventure continued, each chapter of history presenting new obstacles and opportunities. Daniel Thorne, a protector of the past and guardian of the future, faced the tumultuous waves of time with unwavering resolve, determined to preserve the integrity of history and safeguard the course of human progress.

CHAPTER 7: CROSSROADS OF CONFLICT

The journey through time had become Daniel's second nature, each era presenting its own unique challenges. His next mission would take him to one of the most turbulent periods in American history: the American Civil War. The Temporal Order's machinations aimed to exploit the war's chaos, potentially altering its outcome to reshape the future in their favor.

As Daniel arrived in the heart of the Civil War, he was struck by the sheer scale of the conflict. The war had engulfed the nation, its battles and skirmishes painting a vivid picture of struggle and strife. The air was thick with the sounds of cannon fire and the clamor of soldiers, each side fighting with fervor and determination.

His mission was clear: to protect key figures and ensure that the course of the war remained true to its historical trajectory. The Codex Temporis indicated that the Temporal Order sought to manipulate pivotal moments and individuals, aiming to change the course of events for their own gain.

Daniel's primary focus was on President Abraham Lincoln. The Temporal Order's agents had been spotted near key meetings and decision-making processes involving Lincoln. Their goal was to create divisions within the Union leadership, thus weakening the war effort and increasing the chances of a divided and weakened America.

He arrived in Washington, D.C., at a time when the pressures of the war were beginning to mount. Lincoln's leadership was critical, and Daniel knew that his role was to ensure that the President could focus on leading the Union through this dark period.

One evening, Daniel managed to gain access to a private meeting with President Lincoln under the guise of offering support and advice. The meeting took place in a dimly lit room, its walls lined with maps and documents detailing the war's progress.

Lincoln, a tall man with a somber expression, greeted Daniel with a firm handshake. "Mr. Thorne, I understand you have information to share. What can you tell me about our current situation?"

Daniel chose his words carefully. "Mr. President, I have come to offer support and to share insights that may aid in navigating these turbulent times. There are those who seek to undermine your leadership and the Union's efforts."

Lincoln's eyes narrowed with concern. "Undermine us? The situation is dire enough without internal threats. What can we do to counteract this?"

Daniel presented documents detailing covert operations and communications intercepted from the Temporal Order. "These documents indicate that certain factions are working to create discord and weaken the Union's resolve. They aim to exploit the war's chaos for their own ends."

Lincoln reviewed the documents with a frown. "If these claims are true, then we are facing not only a physical battle but a psychological one as well. We must be vigilant and united."

Daniel nodded. "Yes, Mr. President. It is crucial that we maintain unity and focus on the war effort. Any internal division could play into the hands of those who wish to see us fail."

The conversation continued, with Daniel providing insights and strategies to strengthen Lincoln's position. His role was to be a guiding presence, ensuring that Lincoln's leadership remained resolute and effective.

As the days passed, Daniel's work with Lincoln and the Union leadership continued. He worked behind the scenes to bolster morale, counteract disinformation, and support key decisions that would influence the outcome of the war. However, the Temporal Order's agents were always a step behind, their influence still felt in subtle ways.

One night, as Daniel walked through the darkened streets of Washington, he felt a growing sense of unease. The Temporal Order's presence was undeniable, their agents moving in the shadows, seeking opportunities to disrupt the Union's efforts.

Suddenly, Daniel was confronted by Lucius and a group of Temporal Order agents. "You've been quite a thorn in our side, Thorne," Lucius said with a sneer. "Your meddling will come to an end tonight."

Daniel braced himself for the confrontation. The fight was fierce, each blow a testament to the high stakes of their battle. The agents were skilled, but Daniel's determination and knowledge of their tactics allowed him to hold his ground.

In a critical moment, Lucius lunged at Daniel, their struggle intense. "You can't stop us, Daniel. The future we envision is inevitable."

Daniel fought back with equal ferocity. "The future is not set in stone. History belongs to those who fight for its preservation."

With a final, decisive move, Daniel managed to subdue Lucius and the agents, forcing them to retreat. The confrontation had been grueling, but Daniel's victory was a testament to his resolve.

Returning to the monastery, Daniel debriefed Brother Mathias and the Guardians. The report of his mission underscored the ongoing threat posed by the Temporal Order and the importance of remaining vigilant.

"The Civil War was a pivotal moment," Mathias said, his expression thoughtful. "Your efforts have helped maintain the course of history, but the Order's reach is vast. We must continue to strengthen our defenses and support those who work to preserve the integrity of time."

Daniel nodded, his resolve unwavering. "We have faced many challenges, but our mission remains the same. We must protect history and ensure that the Temporal Order's schemes do not alter the course of human progress."

As Daniel prepared for his next journey, the Codex Temporis revealed a new chapter: a critical moment in the rise of the industrial age. The Temporal

Order sought to manipulate this era to control the advancements and reshape the modern world according to their vision.

The adventures of Daniel Thorne continued, each mission a step in the larger battle to protect the past and secure the future. With the Codex Temporis and the unwavering support of the Guardians, Daniel faced each challenge with determination and courage, committed to preserving the course of history and ensuring that the legacy of human progress remained intact.

CHAPTER 8: DAWN OF INNOVATION

The rise of the industrial age was a period of profound transformation, where innovation and progress reshaped the world. For Daniel Thorne, this era presented both an opportunity and a challenge. The Temporal Order sought to manipulate the advancements of this age, influencing key figures and events to secure their vision of the future. Daniel's mission was to protect the integrity of this transformative period and ensure that technological progress continued on its rightful path.

As Daniel arrived in the heart of the industrial revolution, the bustling cities of the late 19th century were a sight to behold. Factories belched smoke into the sky, railways stretched across the land, and the energy of progress was palpable. The era was marked by great strides in technology and industry, but it was also a time of social upheaval and change.

His primary focus was on several key figures whose innovations and leadership would steer the course of industrial progress. Among them was Nikola Tesla, a brilliant inventor whose contributions to electrical engineering were pivotal. The Temporal Order aimed to manipulate Tesla's work, potentially stifling his innovations or redirecting his efforts to serve their own agenda.

Daniel's arrival coincided with a crucial moment in Tesla's career. He had recently begun working on his groundbreaking experiments with alternating current (AC) and wireless transmission. These innovations had the potential to revolutionize the world, and the Temporal Order saw them as a threat to their plans.

Daniel made his way to Tesla's laboratory, a place of wonder and experimentation. The room was filled with the hum of machinery and the crackle of electrical currents, a testament to Tesla's genius. The inventor, with his intense gaze and thoughtful demeanor, welcomed Daniel with a mixture of curiosity and caution.

"Mr. Thorne," Tesla said, extending a hand. "What brings you to my laboratory? I am currently deep in my experiments, and I cannot afford distractions."

Daniel shook Tesla's hand firmly. "I have come to offer my support and to discuss matters of mutual interest. Your work is of great importance, and there are those who seek to undermine it."

Tesla raised an eyebrow. "Undermine it? The progress of science is often met with resistance, but I have always believed in the eventual triumph of innovation."

Daniel nodded. "Indeed. However, there are factions that wish to control or disrupt the course of technological advancement for their own ends. I have information indicating that such factions are targeting your work."

Tesla's expression grew serious. "If what you say is true, then we must act swiftly. My work must proceed without interference. The potential benefits of my inventions are too great to be jeopardized."

Daniel presented Tesla with documents detailing the Temporal Order's attempts to infiltrate his network and sabotage his experiments. "These documents outline their plans and their attempts to manipulate key figures involved in your work. We must remain vigilant."

Tesla reviewed the documents with a frown. "This is troubling news. I had sensed that my work attracted unwanted attention, but I did not realize the extent of the threat. We must ensure that my experiments are protected from those who seek to undermine them."

With Tesla's cooperation, Daniel began working behind the scenes to counteract the Temporal Order's efforts. He helped secure Tesla's laboratory, providing additional resources and support to safeguard his research. The work was intense and demanding, but Daniel's efforts ensured that Tesla's innovations continued to progress unhindered.

Despite their efforts, the Temporal Order's agents were persistent. One evening, as Daniel and Tesla reviewed the latest findings, they were ambushed by a group of agents led by Lucius. The confrontation was immediate and fierce, the agents seeking to disrupt Tesla's work and sabotage their efforts.

"Thorne, you're becoming quite the nuisance," Lucius said with a smirk. "Your interference will not be tolerated."

Daniel stood firm. "I won't allow you to undermine Tesla's work or the progress of this era. The future of humanity depends on the innovations of this time."

The ensuing battle was intense, with Daniel and Tesla defending the laboratory against the agents. The fight was a blend of physical combat and technological marvels, Tesla's inventions providing crucial support. The agents were skilled, but Daniel's determination and Tesla's innovations proved formidable.

In a dramatic moment, Tesla unleashed a surge of electrical energy, temporarily incapacitating the agents and forcing them to retreat. Lucius's eyes burned with fury as he withdrew, promising that this was not the end.

With the immediate threat repelled, Daniel and Tesla returned to their work. The encounter had reinforced their resolve, and they continued to focus on advancing Tesla's research. The work was critical, with each breakthrough bringing the world closer to a new era of technological progress.

As the industrial revolution continued to unfold, Daniel's role remained crucial. He worked tirelessly to support key figures and ensure that the advancements of this age were protected from those who sought to control them. The Codex Temporis guided him through each challenge, providing insights and strategies to counteract the Temporal Order's schemes.

Back at the monastery, Daniel debriefed Brother Mathias and the Guardians on the progress of his mission. The industrial age had been a significant battleground, and their efforts had successfully protected key innovations and ensured that the course of history remained true.

"The industrial revolution was a pivotal moment," Mathias said. "Your efforts have safeguarded the progress of this era, but the Temporal Order's influence is far-reaching. We must remain vigilant and continue to support those who work to preserve the integrity of time."

Daniel nodded, his resolve unwavering. "We have faced many challenges, but our mission remains clear. We must protect history and ensure that the Temporal Order's schemes do not alter the course of human progress."

The Codex Temporis revealed the next chapter of Daniel's journey: a crucial moment in the early 20th century, during a period of social and political upheaval. The Temporal Order sought to exploit this era's divisions and conflicts to further their agenda.

As Daniel prepared for his next mission, he reflected on the challenges he had faced and the battles yet to come. The struggle to protect history and safeguard the future continued, each era presenting new obstacles and opportunities. With the Codex Temporis and the support of the Guardians, Daniel Thorne faced each challenge with determination and courage, committed to preserving the course of history and ensuring that the legacy of human progress remained intact.

CHAPTER 9: ECHOES OF DISSENT

The early 20th century was a period of intense social and political upheaval. The world was grappling with dramatic shifts: the aftermath of the Great War, the rise of new ideologies, and the onset of the Great Depression. For Daniel Thorne, this era represented both a challenge and an opportunity. The Temporal Order aimed to exploit the divisions and instability of this time to further their own ends. It was Daniel's mission to ensure that these transformative years unfolded according to their rightful course.

As Daniel arrived in the vibrant and tumultuous world of the early 20th century, he was struck by the profound changes occurring around him. The cityscape was a mix of grand architecture and burgeoning industrial sites, reflecting the progress and discord of the era. The world was on the brink of a new social order, with ideologies and movements vying for dominance.

His mission centered on key figures who were pivotal in shaping the future during this period. Among them were influential leaders, activists, and thinkers whose decisions and actions would significantly impact the course of history. The Temporal Order sought to manipulate these figures, either by sowing discord among them or by manipulating their ideologies to suit their own agenda.

One of Daniel's primary targets was a prominent social reformer, John Maynard Keynes, whose economic theories were crucial in shaping responses to the Great Depression. The Temporal Order intended to disrupt Keynes's work, potentially undermining efforts to stabilize economies and alleviate suffering.

Daniel first made contact with Keynes during a lecture on economic theory at a university. The hall was filled with eager students and scholars, all eager to hear Keynes's insights on economic recovery. Daniel, blending in as an academic from a foreign country, took a seat among the audience, his eyes fixed on the stage.

After the lecture, Daniel approached Keynes in the

bustling hallway outside. "Mr. Keynes, I greatly appreciated your lecture. Your ideas on economic policy are both innovative and crucial for our times."

Keynes, a man of considerable intellect and charisma, greeted Daniel with a warm smile. "Thank you. The current economic climate demands new thinking and bold actions. What brings you to discuss these ideas with me?"

Daniel chose his words carefully. "I come with a concern. There are forces at work that seek to undermine your efforts and disrupt the progress you advocate. Their goal is to exacerbate the economic crisis for their own benefit."

Keynes's expression grew serious. "Undermine my efforts? That is a grave accusation. What evidence do you have of such interference?"

Daniel handed over documents outlining the Temporal Order's attempts to sabotage Keynes's work. "These documents detail their plans and their attempts to manipulate key economic figures and institutions. It is crucial that your work remains unaffected by these schemes."

Keynes reviewed the documents with a frown. "If these claims are true, then we must be vigilant. The integrity of our economic policies is vital for the recovery and stability of our societies."

With Keynes's cooperation, Daniel worked to protect his economic theories and ensure that his influence remained positive and impactful. They established secure channels for communication and collaboration, fortifying Keynes's efforts against any attempts at interference.

Despite their efforts, the Temporal Order's agents continued to pose a threat. One night, while Daniel was reviewing strategic documents with Keynes, he sensed the presence of the Order's agents. Their intention was clear: to disrupt Keynes's work and create chaos in the economic realm.

Lucius and his agents launched a surprise attack on Keynes's office, their goal to sabotage crucial documents and create confusion. The confrontation was fierce, with Lucius leading the charge. "Thorne, you've been a thorn in our side for too long. This ends tonight."

Daniel braced himself for the battle. "I will not allow you to undermine the progress of this era. The future of countless lives depends on our efforts."

The struggle was intense, with Keynes's office becoming a battleground of ideas and ideology. Daniel fought valiantly, using his knowledge of the Temporal Order's tactics to counter their attacks. The agents were skilled, but Daniel's determination and strategic acumen proved formidable.

In a critical moment, Keynes's support staff, alerted by the commotion, managed to secure critical documents and prevent further damage. Lucius and his agents, seeing their plans thwarted, were forced to retreat, their anger palpable.

With the immediate threat resolved, Daniel and Keynes continued their work, focusing on advancing economic recovery and promoting sound policies. The battle had reaffirmed their resolve and highlighted the importance of their efforts in shaping the future.

Back at the monastery, Daniel debriefed Brother Mathias and the Guardians on the progress of his mission. The early 20th century had proven to be a challenging battleground, but their efforts had successfully protected key figures and ensured that the course of history remained true.

"The early 20th century was a period of great change," Mathias said, his tone thoughtful. "Your efforts have helped preserve the integrity of this era, but the Temporal Order's influence is still a significant threat. We must remain vigilant and continue to support those who work to shape the future positively."

Daniel nodded, his resolve unwavering. "We have faced many challenges, but our mission remains clear. We must protect history and ensure that the

Temporal Order's schemes do not alter the course of human progress."

The Codex Temporis revealed the next chapter of Daniel's journey: a crucial moment in the mid-20th century, during the height of the Cold War. The Temporal Order sought to exploit the tensions and conflicts of this period to further their own agenda.

As Daniel prepared for his next mission, he reflected on the battles he had fought and the challenges yet to come. The struggle to protect history and safeguard the future continued, each era presenting new obstacles and opportunities. With the Codex Temporis and the support of the Guardians, Daniel Thorne faced each challenge with determination and courage, committed to preserving the course of history and ensuring that the legacy of human progress remained intact.

CHAPTER 10: THE COLD WAR CONUNDRUM

The Cold War era was marked by intense geopolitical rivalry, espionage, and ideological conflict. For Daniel Thorne, this period represented a complex and dangerous battleground. The Temporal Order sought to manipulate the tensions of this time to advance their own agenda, threatening to disrupt the delicate balance of global power. Daniel's mission was to navigate these treacherous waters and prevent the Order from altering the course of history.

As Daniel arrived in the mid-20th century, the world was in the grip of Cold War paranoia and conflict. The Berlin Wall stood as a stark symbol of division, and the ideological battle between the United States and the Soviet Union was at its peak. Espionage, political maneuvering, and military posturing defined the era, with both superpowers vying for dominance.

Daniel's mission focused on key figures and events that were pivotal in shaping the course of the Cold War. One of his primary targets was the Cuban Missile Crisis, a critical moment when the world teetered on the brink of nuclear war. The Temporal Order aimed to exploit the crisis to further their own plans, creating chaos and potentially altering the outcome of the conflict.

Daniel's first task was to secure the cooperation of key figures involved in the crisis, including President John F. Kennedy and Soviet Premier Nikita Khrushchev. He needed to ensure that their decisions and actions remained true to history, preventing any manipulation by the Temporal Order.

He began by infiltrating the circles surrounding Kennedy. Under the guise of a foreign advisor, Daniel managed to secure a meeting with the President during a period of intense negotiations. The situation was tense, with the threat of nuclear war looming large.

Kennedy, a man of considerable resolve and intelligence, greeted Daniel with a wary but receptive demeanor. "Mr. Thorne, what can I do for you in these critical times?"

Daniel spoke carefully, aware of the gravity of the situation. "Mr. President, I come with insights that may aid in navigating the current crisis. There are forces at work that seek to manipulate the outcome of this confrontation for their own ends."

Kennedy's expression grew serious. "Manipulate? Our situation is precarious enough without additional threats. What evidence do you have of such interference?"

Daniel presented documents detailing the Temporal Order's attempts to influence key decision-makers and manipulate the flow of information. "These documents outline their plans and their attempts to exploit the crisis to their advantage. It is crucial that we remain united and focused."

Kennedy reviewed the documents with a frown. "If what you say is true, then we must be vigilant. The stakes are too high for us to be distracted by such interference. Our decisions must be based on the best information available and not influenced by outside forces."

With Kennedy's support, Daniel worked behind the scenes to fortify the decision-making process, ensuring that the President's actions were not swayed by external manipulation. He also extended his efforts to Khrushchev, aiming to prevent any disruptions in Soviet responses and maintaining a delicate balance.

Despite their efforts, the Temporal Order's agents continued to pose a threat. One night, while Daniel was assisting with crucial communications, Lucius and a group of agents launched an attack on the secure facility. Their goal was to disrupt the ongoing negotiations and create chaos.

Lucius, with his usual air of arrogance, confronted Daniel. "Thorne, your meddling ends here. We've manipulated enough to ensure our plans succeed."

Daniel stood resolute. "I will not allow you to disrupt the delicate balance of this crisis. The future of countless lives depends on our ability to navigate this period without interference."

The confrontation was fierce, with Daniel and the agents engaged in a high-stakes battle amid the backdrop of tense negotiations. The facility's security systems and communication lines became the focus of the struggle, each side fighting for control over critical information.

In a dramatic moment, Daniel managed to thwart Lucius's attempts to breach secure communications, securing the integrity of the negotiations and ensuring that the President and Premier could continue their discussions without external interference.

With the immediate threat resolved, Daniel continued to support Kennedy and Khrushchev, focusing on maintaining the stability of the crisis and ensuring that their decisions remained true to history. The Cold War was a complex and volatile era, but Daniel's efforts helped safeguard the course of events and prevent the Temporal Order from altering the outcome.

Back at the monastery, Daniel debriefed Brother Mathias and the Guardians on the progress of his mission. The Cold War era had been a critical battleground, and their efforts had successfully preserved the integrity of this period.

"The Cold War was a period of intense conflict and high stakes," Mathias said. "Your efforts have helped maintain the balance of this era, but the Temporal Order's influence remains a significant threat. We must continue to support those who work to navigate these turbulent times."

Daniel nodded, his resolve unwavering. "We have faced many challenges, but our mission remains clear. We must protect history and ensure that the Temporal Order's schemes do not alter the course of human progress."

The Codex Temporis revealed the next chapter of Daniel's journey: a pivotal moment in the late 20th century, during the rise of the digital age. The Temporal Order sought to exploit this era's technological advancements to further their agenda.

As Daniel prepared for his next mission, he reflected on the battles he had fought and the challenges yet to come. The struggle to protect history and safeguard the future continued, each era presenting new obstacles and opportunities. With the Codex Temporis and the support of the Guardians, Daniel Thorne faced each challenge with determination and courage, committed to preserving the course of history and ensuring that the legacy of human progress remained intact.

CHAPTER 11: THE DIGITAL REVOLUTION

The late 20th century ushered in the digital revolution, a transformative era that reshaped how humans communicated, worked, and lived. For Daniel Thorne, this period was both a battleground and an opportunity. The Temporal Order sought to manipulate the rise of digital technology to advance their own agenda, potentially altering the trajectory of technological progress. Daniel's mission was to ensure that the digital age unfolded according to its rightful course, preserving the innovations that would shape the future.

As Daniel arrived in the late 20th century, he was immediately struck by the rapid pace of technological change. Computers and telecommunications were revolutionizing industries and societies, heralding a new era of connectivity and information. The rise of personal computers, the internet, and early digital communication systems marked a pivotal moment in human history.

Daniel's mission focused on key figures and events that were critical in shaping the digital landscape. Among them was Tim Berners-Lee, a computer scientist whose work on the World Wide Web was fundamental to the internet's development. The Temporal Order sought to disrupt Berners-Lee's work, potentially stifling the growth of the web and altering the future of digital communication.

Daniel's first task was to secure Berners-Lee's cooperation and protect his groundbreaking work. He made contact with the scientist at the CERN laboratory in Switzerland, where Berners-Lee was working on his project. The lab was a hub of innovation, with computers and technical equipment scattered throughout.

Berners-Lee, a man with a keen intellect and a vision for the future, greeted Daniel with curiosity. "Mr. Thorne, I understand you have an interest in my work. The development of the World Wide Web is progressing, and we are making significant strides."

Daniel chose his words carefully, aware of the importance of Berners-Lee's work. "Dr. Berners-Lee, I have come to offer my support and to discuss matters of mutual interest. There are forces at work that seek to disrupt your efforts and alter the course of digital innovation."

Berners-Lee raised an eyebrow. "Disrupt my efforts? The digital age is rapidly evolving, but I have not encountered any serious interference. What evidence do you have of such disruption?"

Daniel presented documents detailing the Temporal Order's attempts to undermine the development of the World Wide Web. "These documents outline their plans and their attempts to create obstacles in your work. It is crucial that we maintain the integrity of this project."

Berners-Lee reviewed the documents with concern. "If these claims are accurate, then we must act quickly. The success of the World Wide Web is vital for the future of communication and information. We cannot afford to let external forces derail our progress."

With Berners-Lee's cooperation, Daniel began working behind the scenes to protect his project. They implemented additional security measures and took steps to counteract any attempts at disruption. The work was intense, requiring careful coordination and vigilance to ensure that the development of the web remained on track.

Despite their efforts, the Temporal Order's agents

continued to pose a threat. One night, while Daniel and Berners-Lee were reviewing the latest developments, Lucius and his team of agents launched an attack on the CERN laboratory. Their goal was to sabotage the web's development and create confusion.

Lucius, with his usual air of malice, confronted Daniel. "Thorne, your interference has gone on long enough. We will ensure that the digital revolution is derailed for our benefit."

Daniel stood firm. "I will not allow you to disrupt the progress of this era. The future of global communication depends on the success of the World Wide Web."

The confrontation was intense, with the laboratory becoming a battleground of technology and strategy. Lucius and his agents attempted to compromise key systems and steal critical data. Daniel fought valiantly, using his knowledge of the Temporal Order's tactics to counter their attacks.

In a decisive moment, Berners-Lee utilized his technical expertise to secure the laboratory's systems, preventing further damage and protecting the integrity of his work. Lucius and his agents, realizing their plans had been thwarted, retreated with frustration.

With the immediate threat resolved, Daniel and

Berners-Lee continued their work, focusing on advancing the World Wide Web and ensuring that the project remained on track. The digital revolution was a crucial period in human history, and their efforts helped safeguard the innovations that would shape the future.

Back at the monastery, Daniel debriefed Brother Mathias and the Guardians on the progress of his mission. The late 20th century had proven to be a critical battleground, and their efforts had successfully preserved the integrity of this era.

"The digital revolution was a period of transformative change," Mathias said, his tone reflective. "Your efforts have helped ensure that the course of technological progress remained true, but the Temporal Order's influence is still a significant threat. We must continue to support those who work to shape the future positively."

Daniel nodded, his resolve unwavering. "We have faced many challenges, but our mission remains clear. We must protect history and ensure that the Temporal Order's schemes do not alter the course of human progress."

The Codex Temporis revealed the next chapter of Daniel's journey: a pivotal moment in the 21st century, during a time of global interconnectedness and emerging technologies. The Temporal Order sought to exploit this era's advancements to further their agenda.

As Daniel prepared for his next mission, he reflected on the battles he had fought and the challenges yet to come. The struggle to protect history and safeguard the future continued, each era presenting new obstacles and opportunities. With the Codex Temporis and the support of the Guardians, Daniel Thorne faced each challenge with determination and courage, committed to preserving the course of history and ensuring that the legacy of human progress remained intact.

The journey of Daniel Thorne through the annals of history has been one of immense significance and relentless dedication. Each era he has traversed presented its own unique challenges and opportunities, with the Temporal Order continually seeking to manipulate pivotal moments for their own benefit. Daniel's unwavering commitment to preserving the integrity of history and safeguarding the future has been a testament to his resolve and the principles he stands for.

The Legacy of the Temporal Order

The Temporal Order's attempts to disrupt and control key historical events reveal a complex interplay between ambition and power. Their actions underscore the fragility of historical progress and the ease with which pivotal moments can be altered. By seeking to exploit periods of transformation and upheaval, the Order aims to reshape the future according to their own agenda, often at the cost of countless lives and the broader course of human development.

Daniel's battles against the Order highlight the profound impact that individuals and their decisions can have on the course of history. Each victory against the Order has ensured that the essential currents of progress and innovation remain unimpeded, preserving the path that humanity is meant to follow. His efforts have been crucial in maintaining the balance between progress and manipulation, ensuring that history remains true to its course.

The Importance of Innovation and Integrity

Throughout his journey, Daniel has encountered some of the most transformative figures and events in human history. From the Renaissance and Enlightenment to the Industrial Revolution, the Cold War, and the Digital Revolution, each period has been marked by significant advancements and innovations that have shaped the world as we know it.

Daniel's role in protecting these advancements has underscored the importance of innovation and the integrity of historical processes. By supporting key figures and safeguarding crucial developments, Daniel has ensured that the trajectory of progress remains consistent with its intended path. The preservation of these innovations has had a lasting impact on humanity, influencing the course of future advancements and the overall trajectory of human development.

Reflections on the Journey

Daniel Thorne's journey has been one of remarkable courage and perseverance. Each mission has tested his resolve and required him to navigate complex historical landscapes while combating the interference of the Temporal Order. His success in protecting key moments and figures has been instrumental in ensuring that history unfolds as it should.

The Codex Temporis, as a guiding force, has played a crucial role in Daniel's endeavors, providing him with the knowledge and insights needed to confront the Order's schemes. The support of Brother Mathias and the Guardians has also been vital, offering guidance and resources that have enabled Daniel to fulfill his mission.

As Daniel prepares for the next chapter of his journey, he carries with him the lessons learned from his experiences and the knowledge that his efforts have had a profound impact on the course of history. The struggle to protect the integrity of the past and ensure a positive future is ongoing, with each era presenting new challenges and opportunities.

A Vision for the Future

The story of Daniel Thorne serves as a reminder of the importance of safeguarding history and ensuring that progress remains true to its course. It highlights the need for vigilance and dedication in the face of those who seek to alter the course of events for their own benefit. The preservation of historical integrity is not just about maintaining the past but also about shaping a future that honors the legacy of human achievement and progress.

As the world continues to evolve and face new challenges, the principles and values exemplified by Daniel Thorne remain relevant. His journey underscores the importance of innovation, integrity, and the unwavering commitment to protecting the legacy of human progress. With each era he has defended, Daniel has reaffirmed the belief that the course of history is worth preserving and that the future is shaped by the actions taken today.

The Codex Temporis may reveal new challenges and opportunities, but Daniel Thorne's legacy will endure as a testament to the power of dedication, courage, and the unwavering pursuit of a better future.

www.ingramcontent.com/pod-product-compliance
Lightning Source LLC
Chambersburg PA
CBHW070356230526
45471CB00006B/2590